ALI

A SPARK OF GREATNESS

THE AUTOBIOGRAPHY OF A FIGHTER

WORLD CHAMPION BOXER

LAILA ALI

CALDECOTT HONOREE

COZBI A. CABRERA

Crown Books for Young Readers New York

Are boxers born or made? This is the story of how I became a boxer. My daddy was a boxer. If you look past the ropes, past the title belts, past the bloodline, past the crowds, you'll find a champion forged by fire, long before she entered the ring.

But I'm getting ahead of the story.

I'm Laila. I grow with my big sis Hana, Mommy, Daddy, Samson, and Sheba. Our house has big rooms, tall doors, long hallways, and many people coming and going. Cooks, housekeepers, gardeners, nannies, and all of Daddy's friends, advisers, and admirers.

People are everywhere Daddy goes. Everyone loves him and he loves them.

Yes, Daddy is a boxer, known as the Greatest of All Time. Imagine that! He has speed, grace, and agility in the ring, which means he can "float like a butterfly and sting like a bee," dancing on light feet just out of reach of his opponents. He is also courageous. He speaks out against a war he thinks is unjust, though it isn't a popular opinion.

So, all the world knows about him. Everywhere. Even at lunch. I don't like the spotlight. Would you want to share your daddy with the whole world?

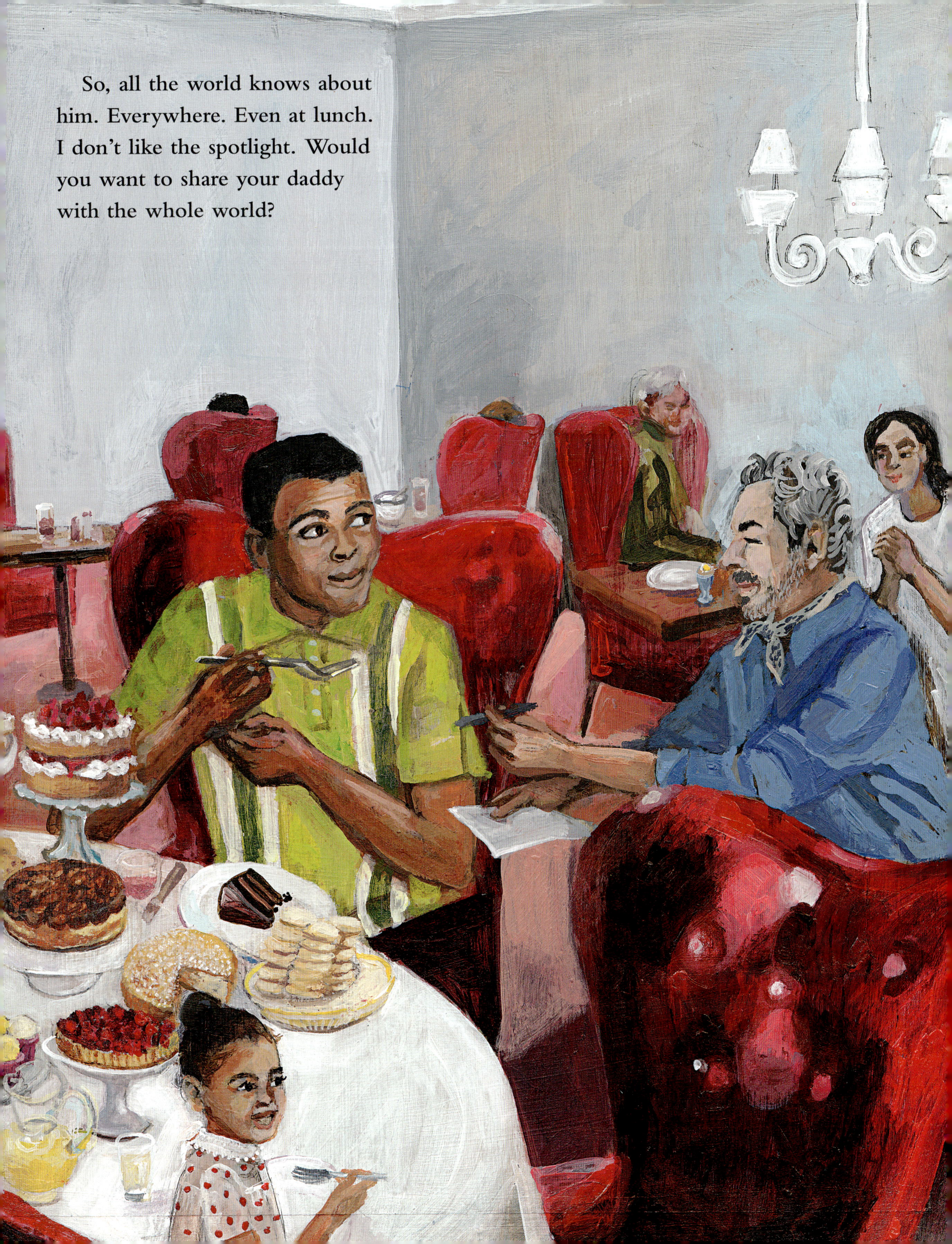

I love to visit the family across the way from my house. They have dinners and watch TV together. Their small house is cozy, and there aren't a whole lot of eyes all over, looking at their lives.

When I get back home, my heart aches. I feel alone.

One day, Mommy, Hana, and I move into a smaller house. Without Daddy. I'm thinking the smaller house will bring closeness like that family across the way. Mommy even gets us a cat I name Madonna. We move again. And again. New schools, new teachers, new friends. Again. There's a wee fire growing in the hollow of me. Sometimes I fight at school.

"What's going on with you?" Mommy asks, Hana by her side. I don't know the answer. Sometimes I fight for Hana, sometimes I step in for someone being bullied, sometimes I fight for myself. Without Daddy at home, somebody's got to be strong.

“You can’t keep fighting like that, Laila,” my teacher says.
“Stop this, Laila!” Mommy says.
But with each breath there’s more smoldering, more fire.

"I want to be independent," I tell Hana. I like that word. If I earn my own money, I can have a home of my own one day that feels just right. So I take classes after school to learn how to give manicures.

Mommy supports what she calls my "ambition" and lends her hands to my creativity and experiments.

But the fire inside me still grows, and there are more fights.

At sixteen, I'm sent to a home for girls who need guidance. I've got chores: making the beds, mopping the floors, cleaning the windows, and helping prepare the meals.

At a group therapy session, one of the girls opens up and tells her story. Then another. There's something about hearing these stories that makes me feel for these girls I just met, that makes me think about how I feel inside.

Maybe there's more to strength than force. I think about this at night when the lights are out. After a day of helping with the chores, listening to and understanding others, I feel different. I hear my mother's voice. It's a lot like floating like a butterfly. Maybe I can use these flames as wings and do good.

One day, a friend and I are watching a big-name men's boxing match on TV. Before the fight is an event I've never seen before: two women boxing.

I watch closely, those women fighting like warriors.

"I can do that." This is what Mommy calls a revelation.

"Do what?"

"Be a boxer," I say.

"Are you crazy, Laila? Look at their faces after this fight! You're way too pretty for all of that! Besides, you've never even played a sport!"

But I know I'm strong. It feels like a match has been lit, like the spark of something new.

I watch Daddy light the torch at the Olympics. All eyes are on him, including mine. I see the fondness for my daddy who loves and helps others, my daddy I've had to share with the world. I see his fire and I see his wings. I picture myself as a world champion, at home in the ring.

Boxing feels right.

Mommy wants to be supportive, though she's concerned. "It's hard to see someone you love hurt. When your daddy fought, it was hard to watch," she says.

But my father doesn't like the idea. "Don't do it," he says. "Baby girl, fighting isn't easy."

"I've made up my mind, Daddy."

He's quiet for a long while, locking eyes with me. He sees the fire in me. If I've got a bit of stubborn in me, he can see that I get it from him.

"Okay, come here. Show me your left jab."

I learn:
to jab correctly,
to move around the ring,
to bob my head out of the
way of an oncoming punch,
to focus on my footwork . . .

. . . to eat like an athlete.

There's a difference between fighting and professional boxing. Boxing requires skill, practice, and discipline. I practice every move until it becomes second nature, until it feels natural.

The six-mile run gets easier. I can see my muscles now. The fire isn't controlling me. My body is learning to obey my mind.

I show up and train. Every day.
No matter what.

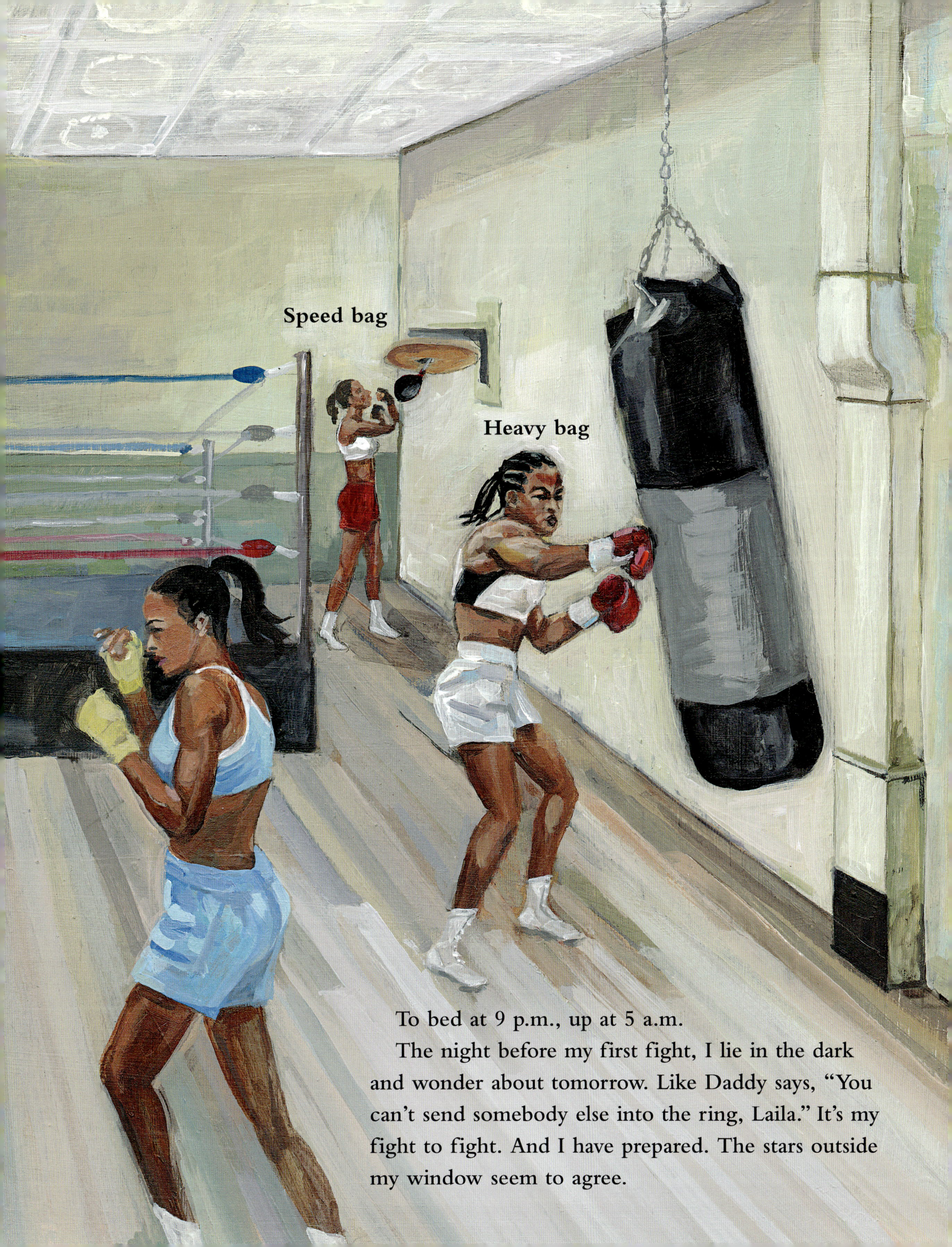

To bed at 9 p.m., up at 5 a.m.

The night before my first fight, I lie in the dark and wonder about tomorrow. Like Daddy says, “You can’t send somebody else into the ring, Laila.” It’s my fight to fight. And I have prepared. The stars outside my window seem to agree.

Now it's time to enter the ring. I've worked for this: My hands are wrapped, my gloves are on, I'm ready to face the world. I look straight ahead and climb into the ring, focused and confident, feeling the crowd's energy. The bulbs are flashing; the crowd is chanting, "Ali, Ali!"

I can feel the confidence in my step that comes with preparation and skill, with embracing and commanding this fire, my fire. I've had a lot of practice all these years, fighting the flames inside me. Now I'm using my fire.

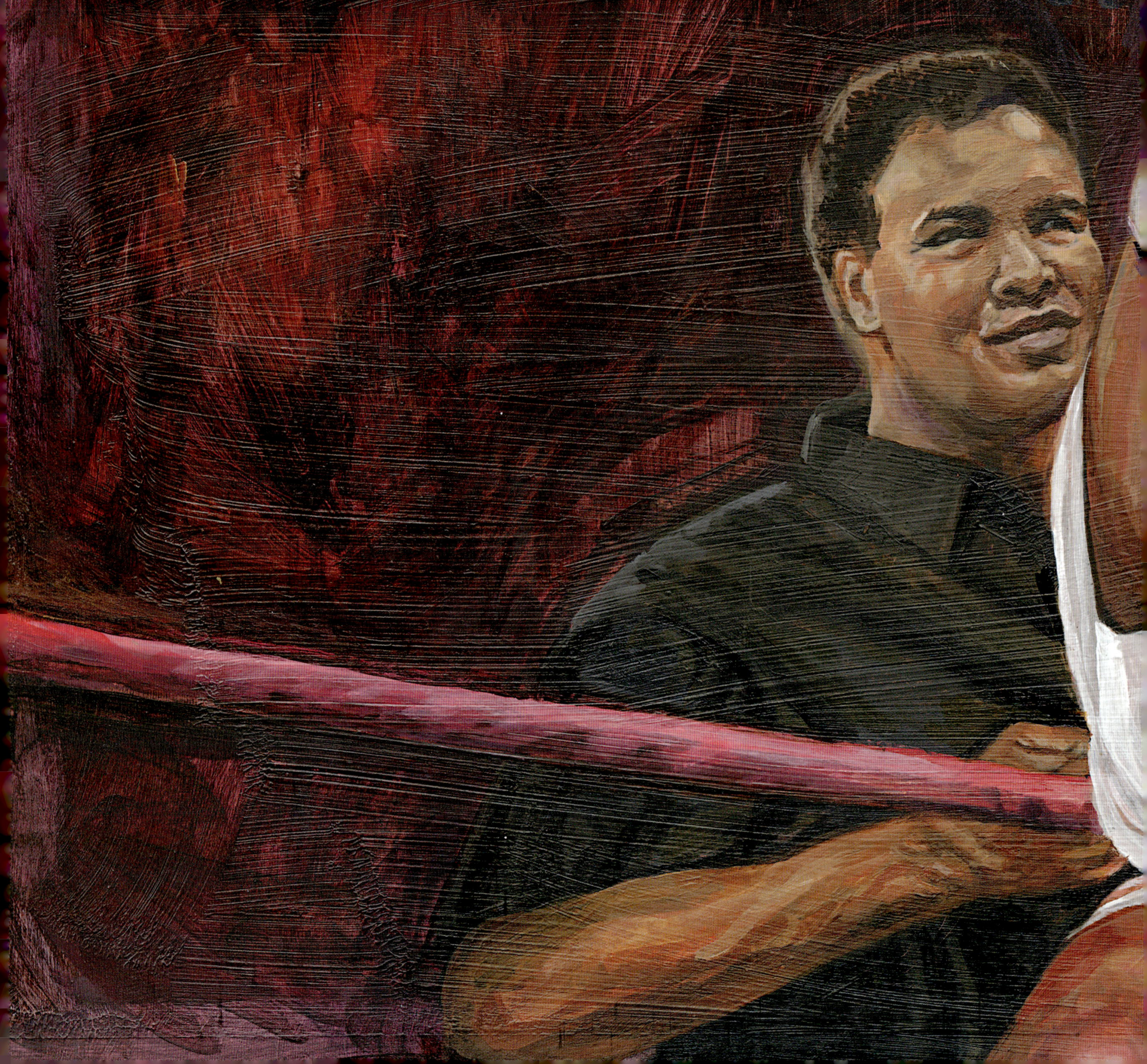

ALI

And there's my daddy at ringside, bursting with pride. The bell rings, I meet my opponent in the middle. I rapid-fire my left-right combinations, some quick, hard uppercuts, and see her stagger against the ropes.

TURNIN

The fight is over in fifty-four seconds!
I win my first match by knockout!
“Ali! Ali! Ali!” is the cry.

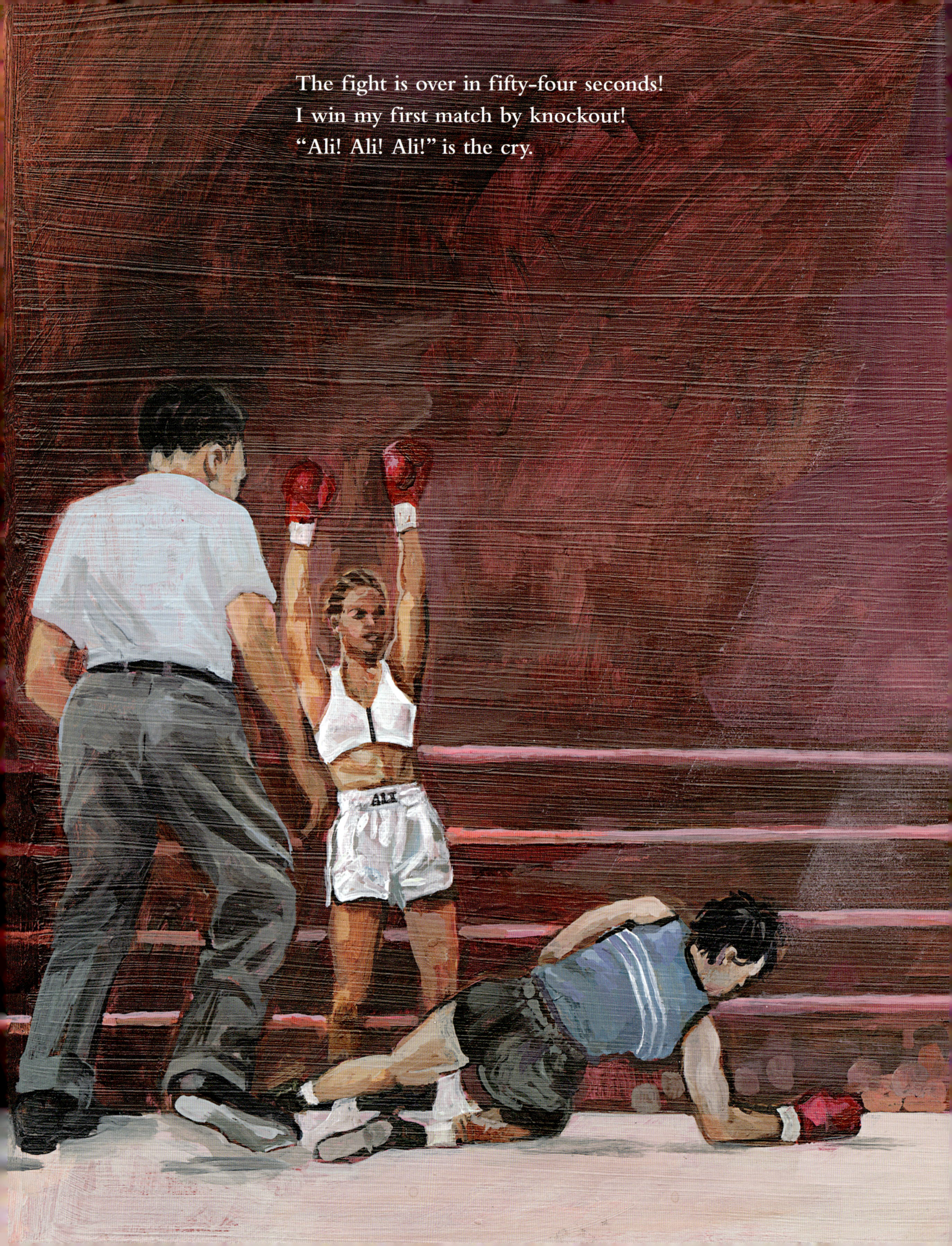

A fire still burns in me. I'm a champion because I use it for good. It's my very own superpower. It makes me stronger, fearless, confident, unstoppable, driven, empowered, and complete. Is there a fire in you?

A NOTE FROM THE AUTHOR

When I stepped into the boxing ring for the first time, I didn't just win that fight—I discovered my power. From that night on, I never lost a match. I finished my boxing career undefeated, with 24 wins—21 of them by knockout—and became a five-time world champion. I even made history as the first woman to give expert boxing commentary during the Olympic Games, in 2012! And in 2022, I was honored to be inducted into the International Boxing Hall of Fame. But my story doesn't stop there.

These days, I still bring the heat—but now it's in the kitchen! I've loved cooking since I was ten years old, inspired by my grandmother's delicious Creole dishes and my passion for creating healthy, flavorful meals. I believe food is the foundation of a strong, vibrant life, and I share that message in my cookbook *Food for Life*.

Just like my dad, Muhammad Ali, I believe in giving back. I work with organizations that support equality, health, and community—like the Women's Sports Foundation, the American Heart Association, the American Diabetes Association, Feeding America, and Peace4Kids. Helping others live healthier and happier lives is part of what keeps my own fire burning.

Today, I live in Georgia with my husband, Curtis, and our two children, Curtis Jr. and Sydney. Being a mother is one of my greatest joys, and it reminds me every day how important it is to be a positive role model—not only for my own kids but for all the young people coming up behind me.

My journey hasn't always been easy, but I've learned that confidence, faith, and believing in yourself can carry you farther than you ever imagined. Never let anyone tell you what you can't do. Listen to your heart, stay true to who you are, and let your own light shine bright.

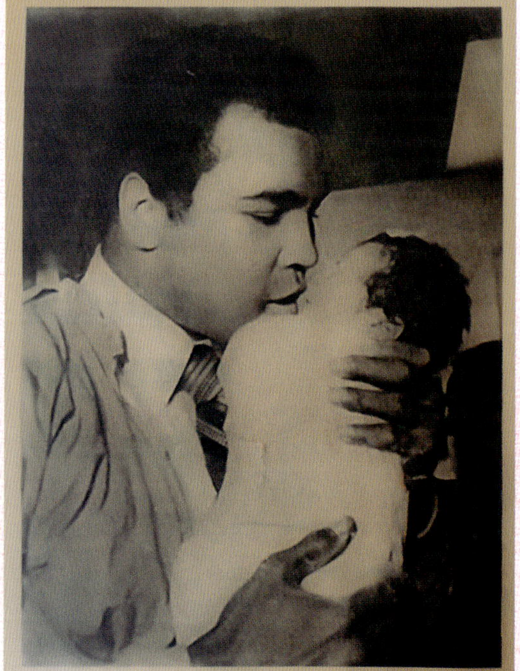

Photo by Marice Cohn)

The next champ (?)

Heavyweight champion Muhammed Ali has a new contender in his family, but the baby won't be any competition for him in the ring — she's a 7-pound-10-ounce girl. Ali's wife, Veronica, gave birth at 10:20 a.m. Friday at Mount Sinai hospital, where "mother and daughter are doing fine," a spokesman said. Ali is training on Miami Beach for his next fight.

Mikki Willis

BOXING CAREER FACTS

Professional Record: 24 wins, 0 losses (21 knockouts)

Years Active: 1999–2007

Weight Classes: Super Middleweight and Light Heavyweight

WORLD CHAMPIONSHIPS

• WBC Super Middleweight Champion • WIBA Super Middleweight Champion
• IWBF Super Middleweight Champion • IBA Super Middleweight Champion
• IWBF Light Heavyweight Champion

HALL OF FAME HONORS

• International Women's Boxing Hall of Fame—Class of 2015
• Nevada Boxing Hall of Fame—Class of 2018
• International Boxing Hall of Fame—Class of 2021

For my daughter, Sydney—may you always see the strength, brilliance, and power within you. And for every young girl who's ever been told she couldn't—let this be proof that she can. —L.A.

To all our readers, young and not so young, who will find their courage —C.A.C.

Crown Books for Young Readers • An imprint of Random House Children's Books
A division of Penguin Random House LLC, 1745 Broadway, New York, NY 10019
penguinrandomhouse.com • rhcbooks.com

Editor: Kelly Delaney • Designer: Jan Gerardi • Copy Editors: Melinda Ackell and Patricia Callahan
Managing Editor: Tisha Paul • Production Manager: Jennifer Moreno
Library of Congress Cataloging-in-Publication Data is available upon request.
ISBN 978-0-593-43485-7 (trade) — ISBN 978-0-593-43486-4 (lib. bdg.) — ISBN 978-0-593-43487-1 (ebook)
The text of this book is set in 16-point Bembo MT Pro Semibold. The illustrations were created using acrylics on gessoed illustration board.
Manufactured in China 10 9 8 7 6 5 4 3 2 1
The authorized representative in the EU for product safety and compliance is Penguin Random House Ireland, Morrison Chambers, 32 Nassau Street, Dublin D02 YH68, Ireland, https://eu-contact.penguin.ie.
Random House Children's Books supports the First Amendment and celebrates the right to read.